MW01093857

# THE
# MIGRANT STATES

## Books and Music by Indran Amirthanayagam

*The Elephants of Reckoning*, Hanging Loose Press, New York, 1993

*Ceylon R.I.P.,* Institute for Ethnic Studies, Colombo, Sri Lanka 2001

*El infierno de los pajaros*, Editorial Resistencia, Mexico City, Mexico, 2001

*El hombre que recoge nidos*, Editorial Resistencia/Conarte, Monterrey, Mexico, 2005

*The Splintered Face* (Tsunami Poems), Hanging Loose Press, New York 2008

*Sol Camuflado*, Lustra Editores, Lima, 2010

*La pelota del pulpo* (The Octopus's Ball), Editorial Apogeo, Lima, 2012

*Sin adorno: lirica para tiempos neobarrocos*, University Autonoma de Nuevo Leon, Mexico 2012

*Uncivil War,* Tsar (now Mawenzi House), Toronto, 2013

*Aller-Retour Au Bord de la Mer,* Legs Editions, Haiti. 2014

*Pwezi a Kat Men* (written with Alex LaGuerre), Edition Delince, Miami, 2017

*Il n'est de solitude que l'ile lointaine*, Legs Editions, Haiti, 2017

*Coconuts On Mars*, Poetrywala, Paperwall Publishers, Mumbai, India, 2019

*En busca de posada*, Editorial Apogeo, Lima, Peru, 2019

*Paolo 9*, Manofalsa, Lima, Peru, 2019


*Rankont Dout*, CD with Donaldzie Theodore, Pawol Tanbou, Titi Congo. Port Au Prince. October 2017

*They Died Not in Vain*, music video, with Evans Okan, Cuernavaca, November 2019

# THE
# MIGRANT STATES

Indran Amirthanayagam

Hanging Loose Press,
Brooklyn, New York

Copyright © 2020 by Indran Amirthanayagam

Published by Hanging Loose Press, 231 Wyckoff Street, Brooklyn, New York 11217-2208. All rights reserved. No part of this book may be reproduced without the publisher's written permission, except for brief quotations in reviews.

www.hangingloosepress.com
Printed in the United States of America 10 9 8 7 6 5 4 3 2 1

Hanging Loose Press thanks the Literature Program of
the New York State Council on the Arts for a grant in support of
the publication of this book.

Cover art and design: Anandan Amirthanayagam
Text design: Nanako Inoue
Author photo: Val Loh

**Acknowledgments**
Earlier versions of some of these poems were published in *Haiti en Marche, Hanging Loose,* and *A World Without Wars.*

ISBN 978-1-934909-63-8

*"What happens to a dream deferred?*
*—Langston Hughes*

For the migrants,

For Guy and Indrani Amirthanayagam.

For my brother Revantha
who provoked us to set off
on the journey to the other side.

For Anandan  and Lola.

For Kimberly.

For all the residents
of my heart, who inspire me
to write, who feed me
the energy of eternal delight.

# Preface

Migrants are on the move, while our Earth is staggering, roiling and rolling, drunk on human breath. We are living in the middle of the Emergency and some of us will not be able to escape. The seas rise and boil. Brush fires move at a lightning clip. Heavy, sooty swats of Delhi air penetrate masks and decorum, silting lungs with a slow accumulation of poisons— as if our lungs, the breathing tubes, the bellows of our lives, have become a burial pit, the sand thrown in. So what does the Migrant state?

Two hundred years after Walt Whitman set off from Paumanok, this is what his descendants find along the road: Democracy sputters, stutters. Can we survive the current, surreal comedy where words, the raw material of poetry, have been spun, propagated as propaganda that threatens, as Orwell predicted, to make lies into truth, war into peace? I would add the jobs of reporter, poet, witness—as suspect now as they were in Plato's mind when he tried to create his exclusive Republic.

Yet I admire Plato because I champion free speech, the free mind. Let him have his Republic: only let me state my poetry. We need open borders everywhere, open borders of the mind, of languages. We need to cross over at ports of entry with our dances, tongues, poems and gods. So pack your bag for the trip. I invite you to put these poems in an outer pouch, easy to grab and show at Customs.

In my words, Sir, there are no vegetable products, no animal residues, no contraband. They are here to wake up essences, dreams, memories; to tell stories of where people come from, and the disputes, struggles, successes they encounter along the way.

And they offer an affirming flame, attempt to speak truth to power, and, I believe, can be useful in the most important fight of our time: that of reducing our footprint, our ecological stain. We must take care of air, water and earth, become really worthy stewards. We must care for all other living beings with whom we share the ecosystem. We are not kings or dictators. And thankfully, we have a system—that least bad of systems, according to Mario Vargas Llosa, but ours, the one Whitman discovered walking abroad from Paumanok, the one these poems reaffirm, in these migrant states.

—Indran Amirthanayagam

# CONTENTS

CONTENTS

## Mind Breathing

I have missed *Mind Breaths* left by accident at a bus stop
in Waialae Kahala in 1979—two years earlier I heard
Allen Ginsberg sing "Father Death Blues" from the manuscript.

On November 17, 1960 I breathed for the first time without
maternal assistance, on a cot, at Macarthy Nursing Home,
a few blocks from our residence in Colombo.

Allen brought a harmonium as a carry-on music box
on his flight to Oahu.  Back then nobody examined
strings for chemical traces, death marches, laments.

My most treasured documents, letters from Allen
to my father, painting by Jose Luis Cuevas that graced
the front cover of my first Spanish book,

comment from a certain President Clinton about
the tsunami and poetry, together in a file that disappeared
in 2006 after our house was ransacked by unidentified

human beings in search of food, drink, money
and letters written by the author of *Mind Breaths*.
This is not a joke. I bear witness to these losses

here as my own attempts to speak, in breaths,
shall infuse a poem able still to coagulate, distill,
strain a few thousand disparate disappearances into verse.

Friends and readers, hypocrites (I love associating
with the most damned, dramatic traditions) and Saints —
Francis, whom I embraced at confirmation, and many

other inspiring staffs — for each day and hour
of our persistent walking ahead in spite of inclement
accidents, robberies, forgetfulness, come and drink.

## This Is No Time For Criticism

I realize my lines are not lyrical. They have no surprising leaps,
or rhythmic epiphanies. They are flat, a body shot on the street
visited by paramedics, wailing young men and women. We do
not discriminate in 2019. We are witnessing birth of a revolt,
a rejection, and you say my verse is agitprop, an unfit exercise
for poetry. I reply writing, that the body must be buried with dignity,
and surviving family paid; as for the healing of decades-old wounds
opened up again by a tank trundling into the center of the city,
I offer my pen as a bullet-proof vest, immune to criticism,
resistant like an ear of wheat in the wind, an eagle brushing
off the fur of a mouse from its wings. Who is looking down
on us now, my friend? Who is saying shut the bloody
fuck up and write truly hermetic poetry?

FOR WALT

## Stop By

You said stop by, spend the day and night and I would possess the origin
of all poems. Well here I stand, and I am willing to pay any price, give
of the apple, sign a mortgage, a revolving credit line,
and jump on the disaffected bomber about to set off his vest. Let's roll.
"Damn doors. Damn jambs." "Raise high the roof beams." "Call me Ahab."
"I have seen the best minds." "When I from black, and he from white cloud free."
I am in your debt, Walt, and to all the poets who gave birth to you and to those
you have sired in turn. Thank you. The word is good and in our hands now.

****

## After Midnight

Walter Whitman will come out of his mother's ninth month midnight
tomorrow, the 31st of May, in the family room, at the Walter Whitman
home in West Hills, Huntington, Long Island, to be known henceforth
in all poetry as Paumanok, the birth island of the poet who at eleven
years old left formal schooling for the school of the road, learning
printing and the journalistic arts, most of all learning how to observe
closely the tiniest movement in a blade of grass, and the rustle
of a bird in the bush, and the rush of wind as the bird and flock
took off from the marsh and into this brief ode, spoken at a turn,
a crossing point before tomorrow which will never be today
nor the day after, nor next week, nor back in time
to Huntington, on May 30th 1819 when Walt, a hairy,
blind baby, was just one day away from bawling into light.

****

## Walt, 200

Break the locks, unleash the mind. Walt Whitman has left Paumanok.
He is abroad. He is sitting among us, in our soul. He flies the post
with pigeons and the giant freight planes. He hops freight trains
and rides into Mexico. He is on a P & O Cruise visiting Saint Kitts
and Barbados. He has joined the merchant marine. He sails
into Guantanamo. He throws fish into the sea in search of whales.
He has the biggest, longest beard in the world. He jives, thrives,
cavorts, shimmers. He is two hundred years old today and he does
not give a flying rat. He is in your mind Mr. President even if you cannot
smother or scratch or squeeze him out. He is gloriously spirit, gadfly, rabbit
and sloth. He nurses our democratic wounds. He knows how to write
history from the pebble's view, the side glance of the wren, the snake
hanging in the tree. He is black and white and all shades of grey. He is
our friend and guide and he will elect us every time we fall down. Let us
go back to Paumanok with what we've learned these two hundred years.
Let us go back to set forth again, Walt Whitman in our backpack.

****

## Ode to and from Whitman

Ezra said you were pig-headed but he recognized that you made
  the new wood. We have been
carving for more than 150 years since you first painted the leaves
  of grass. Now, we have
plastics on our mind, floating islands of waste, stuffing stomachs of fish and
  whales, weighing
a third of all fish in the sea, and by 2050 even more than all of those fish.
  What would Walt
say now? Turn his attention to water, to streams and rivulets, rivers and
  lakes, spilling into
the plastic-ridden sea. What would he say about the inheritance of
  Roosevelt? Who is turning
in his bed? Would he monitor delivery of babies, sailing out of
  the birth canal, the ninth
month midnight, to be abandoned at a hospital door, in the alleyway
  of Walmart, by a young
mother driven mad with anxiety, guilt, shame and fear? Would he
  say that the mother

can murder and create? Would he say that if that mother had
        the right to choose, and the means,
she should be allowed to stop cells multiplying before they become embryos
        or further along
open eyes and start to taste spices consumed by their host? Roe versus
        Wade. Whitman
is grand. Contains multitudes. He did not reject the Negro or
        prostitute. He saw Man and God
in a blade of grass. This poem is for a panel on Pan. On nature. On
        the transcendent spirit.
God or sprite. Wood genie. What courses through the blood of a stevedore
        and a banker, a rabbit
and a leaping hare, a sloth and a panther? Life, yes, and impending
        death. Imagine driving
along a highway, at seventy miles an hour. You must have thought,
        at least once, what if
you swerved, into the guard rail, to escape a deer, across the median
        into incoming traffic?
To kill oneself. To be killed. To have the hand on the button of
        your own desire and fate.
I am large. I contain multitudes. I will roar through this life
        and will not stop until I stop.
Moloch be damned. The military industrial complex be
        damned. America, go bother
somebody else. I have more than two dollars in my pocket but I am
        not satisfied with a coffee
at Starbuck's. This is a relative poem, an allusive child, an homage
        and a diversion. Can
you spot the antecedents? Or shall we protest again in our time so he from
        black and I
from white cloud free? The old arguments and quarrels course still
        through our psyches.
Walt is contemporary as a blade of grass, a cow allowed to
        chew its cud in a field,
an organic tomato, a wild mushroom. Walt is relevant as
        a raw food juice designed
to pick you up every morning, to say you can go local, bring
        the chains of distribution home.
You can go abroad and walk to the greengrocer. Live
        in the world and in a small
space of earth to learn to bear the beams of love.
        William Blake gave us that adage.

Walt said *there was never more inception than there is now,*
    *nor any more youth or age*
*than there is now, and will never be any more perfection than there is now, not*
*any more heaven or hell than there is now.*

# CURTAIN CALL

# Prelude

To live on the island
satisfied basic needs:
poetry readings
in the evenings, noodled
curries, belly dancing,
and love, and gardens,

famous writers on street-
corners, monuments,
chestnuts, ice and
hibiscus, movies
filmed in the fruit market
and paintings

in grand salons, and
love, and smacking
bites of a burger
with a pint, the jeweled
eye of a fish, a tailor
who survived the number

branded on his arm,
the delight of lingering
over a glass of wine,
a chat, in love,
sunrise and sunset
over two splendid rivers.

# Marked

I write to all corners of the far-flung universe
yet some critics remind me of the emphasis
I place on the birth island and its follies.

They ask me, why I don't move elsewhere.
Surely, life is there, and that road of excess
which should take me to the palace where

I can seduce the princess and settle down
with a few hundred servants; but I will not
be content with the lord's life, I am a worker

bee, better yet an engineer supervising
refocusing a river, moving its channel
towards new and expectant fields full

of maidens, shoots and mewling lambs,
but stuck by the force of the river's original
impulse to course according to its ancient design

that does not depend on Man or free will
or immigrant desire, no matter what I do or where
I write the tale etched on my forehead.

# Until Death

The world might end tonight, better
write, get into the back end of the closet
and pull out old jumpers and bow ties,

burrow into floorboards and pick up
a few pins and stickers; your daughter
will be pleased that her father remembers

such details; look hard for phone
numbers of great, dead poets, who shaped
your life, who remain counselors.

Mingle with dust and find the lost
poems of 1976, when you began
to compose verses at a fevered pace,

every day a new poem, and your father
correcting each one, and his friend
Reuel Denney said you had mastered

the four-beat line, and three years
later you were fronting a punk band
screaming four-beat boogie, and

I think that is enough autobiography
for this poem which cannot end
but in writing or dying.

## Recalling Sunday

I have fought the blues on so many
Sundays I have lost count of hours frittered
away in sifting through the past
to understand why I carry a peculiar strain

of melancholy that pierces all activity
and must in the end be endured, tempered
by the Mass, a story shared at evening
with my daughter, a cricket game

relived fondly when far removed from
the pitch—and dare I say it—in company
of that bitch, Life, who does not spare
even Sunday to poke a dagger into memory.

## Flown Away

This minced meat,  keema
mixed with rice and peas
and a cup of milk tea, Pakistan

brought home with raita
and good company
at Shant Cottage, Kent, where

the proprietor asked me
to focus—on the tips of leaves,
birds' nests in high branches,

where new blackbirds
will fly— not on roots preserved
in the jewelry box, shaved

nails, hair locks,
that the muddy river
and its squealing fowl

no longer form a part
of the English body, free,
yet pleased to eat this meal,

to share a bit of Pakistan
with a prodigal son
who stopped by to chat

far from his island
home, Ceylon,
rubbed off the map.


Note: *Ceylon was the name of the island when I popped
out of my mother's womb in 1960*

## Batting, in Love

I enjoyed captaincy, devoting
myself to strategy, batting order,
resting my star fast bowler,
moving fielders frequently
to unsettle batsmen, keep
them looking to place shots.

This focus on the game
and my team filled weekends
and leisure hours. We wanted
to excel despite our hodge-podge
of migrant cricketers and Americans
who learned the game at college

under guidance of coach Kamran,
who kept wicket and batted
with Imran, Majid and Mushtaq
at university in Pakistan before
emigrating to the United States
and a new career opening bowling

on the American team. We were
lucky to have him shaping
our adolescent arms. I was only
17 when I arrived at the college.
Would I have continued
playing cricket back in Ceylon?

What a commitment of time
to try out for the First Eleven,
like acting, another victim of
the impulse to study, prepare
a career. Girls somehow did not
disturb concentration back then.

Amazing to try and recreate
that sensation of wholeness
before inevitable infatuation,
leaping desire, love and attendant
heartbreak and loneliness.
If we could just play cricket

until we become old, and retire
then to lawn bowling or golf,
keeping frailty, tenderness
and despair awakened
by love at arm's length, yet
when and where were we pricked

to fall in love with our game?

## Cricket Match, Cope Field

*We are coming in from the cold.* I remember, raised
on my teammates' shoulders, how I was carried off
the field. We had won. We had won, finished the season
streaking victorious. We felt good. We had overcome
obstacles facing our hodge-podge side, half of which
had learned to play cricket at the college late in life. *Coming in,*
*Coming in.* Beer cans were popping that evening, Marley
blasting on the record player. We danced. We danced.
I was the captain. I had my glasses knocked off
my nose by a ball early that Spring. I was dizzy, saw a sky
full of lights. But I got up. I got up. Then spent my energy
over the rest of the season, winning with talents under
my command. I was right. I was right. The team played
fine, fine. I could put myself down the order, face slower
bowling. It was all right. It was all right. Proverbs smacked
fours and sixers all over the field. We danced. We danced.
Underwood bowled the yorker. We laughed and cried. Kamran,
our coach, cooked Pakistani delights at his home to celebrate.
Even now a chai and a chappal kabab taste like victory.

## When I Left Punk and Took Holy Orders

The punk scene drew me in when I turned nineteen,
the discordant strum, strutting about stage
like a rooster at dawn. I loved flinging music
in everybody's face but remained unaware
of sex and drugs. Abstemious I was, most
dangerous for my absolute sense of purpose.
I had Kissinger, the Lone Ranger, to throw
off his horse, Margaret Thatcher, the Iron
Maiden, to stomp upon with my adolescent
yearning. I was a Laborite, of course, committed
to the working toff, not some Conservative
blue nose smelling Maggie's bum. But my angst
drove deeper into history, unleashing desire
against the powerful, mostly women—Cleopatra,
the Queen of Sheba—although I extended my attacks
to corporations and dictators. But what did I build?
The band dropped me for my original songs. They
wanted to play covers, earn a bit at parties, They made
excuses. I cried quietly turning rage into shame,
became a scribe then in the monastery of poetry.

## The Dike Broke

The dike broke, sand bags crumbled
and water flowed into my computer
washing away all the pictures and poems,
and now that I am dry and facing

a new bed I wonder how shall I nourish
the seeds you furnish without returning
to the waters to salvage some instrument
that kept its hide like these tablas tapping

the morning on the Tamil Service. Surely,
a man is not a cat, that he must make
amends with his life, prepare the bed
with his heart and memory? Make it new,

his maestro remarked. Renew, renew
chimed the songbirds in chorus.

## Musicians in Exile

*—David, we must talk.*

I too founded a punk band with my best friends. We called
ourselves The End. The last time we played together
was 1981. In the basement of a dorm at Haverford College.

We also have a close buddy, Colin Potts, who wrote two of the songs.
He is a tourist guide in Chester, England. The lead guitarist Sig,
of Latvian and Connecticut stock, plays guitar at night in Berlin.

Richard, the one-man band, Brautigan his guru, lives now
in Hong Kong where he banks and jots anarchic wit in social media
blasts. Kenny drums in South Florida after doctoring during the day.

And I write poems, sometimes lyrics, and dream that we will play
together again before the Reaper claps, and Lazarus closes his book,
to those who gave up the game, the good fight, to eliminate the DMZ,

the Wall, to bring the End back to the beginning where the body
is wiry, the hair long, and the dream fresh in the shot glass
on the counter at Roach & O'Brien's, in the glass hanging

on Mrs. William Burroughs' head . . . wrong myth. We were Quakers,
pacifists, back then. Not sure now. We have not spoken in a while.
Once a Quaker always a Quaker. Once a bum, rolling musical wheel,

talking drum, nobody can shut us up. Nobody can say the End
will die again. Not in this poem. Not on stages of Berlin
or Hong Kong. Not in Washington D.C where I publish this call

for tryouts. The production will be grand, cover the planet.
We want versatile and committed actors who sing, dance, play
drums, guitars, cowbells, who find pleasure even in exile.

## Curtain Call
*—for A.P.David*

When you please, make the reader laugh, lighten
the baggage he carries around home, street and
office, you reach the first level of enlightenment,
then you pause, consulting the poets along
the way. Yeats wrote what then, Cavafy offered

that you cannot escape the city in which
you were born, Nazim dreamed of a straw blonde,
a night train across Europe, poplars falling
in the Turkey from which he remained in exile.
Exile is the modern condition, Ceylon felled

like a poplar, but how did Java vanish,
or British Honduras? I feel a need to inform
myself of what is passing down the slide
in Belize, around the *rijsttafel.* I used to taste
marmite on my tongue, jellied eels, kippers, mash,

but I am not returning to England this Christmas,
the journey longer and deeper, up the coast,
to Jaffna, where Pappa had wanted to go
on foot after the stroke, pottering about
the house in Colombo, and we held him back.

The impossible return. My brother David says,
*one goes awkwardly to meet oneself. And she*
*speaks gibberish back.* I do not resist the urge
to borrow his line. At this stage of life,
individual ambition is a bit silly, like Lear

amusing himself with his one hundred
knights in the homes of his dissembling eldest
daughters. He learned his lesson, found
his reckoning on the moor. I hear myself
saying, just the gratitude is the rub.

I will love you *according to my bond,*
*no more, no less.* Cordelia spoke truth,
my brother too. Bring Ceylon back on stage,

a revival, limited engagement. Furnish
the set with poplars and palmyras.

Let there be peace accords signed
every night before a roaring house. Open
admission. Even dictators may take
their seats. But they will not, of course.
They will not be allowed to sit in peace.

Ghosts will rise from the trap door, stride
in from stage left and right. The proscenium
will break down into theater in the round
and actors will take charge of fate if only
for the length of the curtain call.

## English Migrant

I am digging into English memory,
Barbara Earle's class, Wordsworth
and daffodils, trying out for
*Twelfth Night* and casting

as ship captain and priest,
minor characters not related
to the play's leading families,
a sensitive point for a Tamil

boy unaware of his extreme
solitude added to his wish
to belong, to graft himself
upon the American tree,

but Ms. Earle helped me
along, selecting me later
as the lawyer in the Senior
Variety Show, a major role

in front of the entire school,
a speaking part in a musical,
tweed-blazered, spectacled
and English-accented

in an America that respected
the Queen's English
even more than her subjects,
a strange yet minor twist

to more than 200 years
of independence
and development
of *the special relationship*,

and now where
did I intend to stroll
among the daffodils
reading the Lake Poets

in Honolulu under
palm trees, by the Pacific,
eating guavas and mangos,
wearing slippers . . .

the wonderful life
of the English scholar
in the tropics,
comforted

by the poetry
even if the flora
did not correspond
to the melody?

I became a citizen
and learned later
from Whitman
that America

contains a
contradictory
brimming multitude,
which Lorca discovered

as well when he walked
downtown from Columbia
the year of the Great Crash
writing *Poeta en Nueva York*.

# Beating

I learned in America to pursue citizenship
like a lightning bug flitting about in the garden,
moving down to the street, crossing over
the neighbor's fence.  "Good fences don't make

good neighbors" my parents taught  me reciting
Frost and Eliot while serving spiced sambols
and string hoppers, I became the Western
Oriental Gentleman, the many-layered human

strengthened by parental support of border-
crossing, of landing in proverbial America.
I don't know who young people read now,
except for Ginsberg, and who they will consult

in the future, at the Library of Congress,
when this poem goes off the road, spins
wheels in the mud until it is abandoned
and the traveller resumes his journey on foot,

discovering elm and birch, if the accident
happens to occur in New England, and if
I manage to dash across the lower 48 states
I could leave my baggage beside a redwood.

# The Persistence of Popular Culture

I have lost my way, Spock.
I am tiny and effervescent;
I am getting older and older,
I wish now to call in chips, Spock.

Give me the elixir that furnished
your extremely long ears and
mathematical brow, Spock.
Now is the time to count

galaxies while we transfer
coordinates.  Are you
in this universe to stay, Spock?
Have you become Man?

Do you speak English?  Are
you merely an actor?  Is Nimoy
a code word  for Yomin?
Who are you, Leonard?

## Written in Advance

*Thank you but I am alarmed alarmed .*
*To be hospitalized is no small thing*—Grace Cavalieri

Yes, I understand and I was surprised I had
to stay the night. But there were compensations
for that elevated troponin in one take of blood,
I met the night nurses, who are tender and clear
guides, then the hospital kitchen provides low
cholesterol food, roast turkey, mashed potatoes,
which I don't usually eat but associate
with the heart of this great land,
and my favorite feast, Thanksgiving.

I have supported wild turkey conservation
and forgiveness of the bird at the White House,
but have eaten farm-raised cousins with relish
and without guilt. So I eat fowl and fish
in keeping with Biblical tradition, and baby lamb
from New Zealand, but am shifting away
from cow. Eventually I will become Hindu
too, a syncretic poet, lover of all World religions
and its poetry and song. Well, not every singer,

not every song. But there is enough grand music
to go, you said it, round, round. There is enough
love, say it, to beat spears and swords, into putty,
ploughshares, the United Nations. Let us not forget
ideals driving the coming together. Let us revive
that body politic. Let us dance possessed
and scream, peace, baby, on earth, among
all living things. Peace, Mr. Police I lie down
at your feet, petals in my hair. Drink my scent

before you make your arrest, before you take
me away in that van with sirens and chains.
Yes, off with the nuisance but listen to me
deep in your soul. I will have my day in court.
and on the street. I will be heard in the halls
of the hospital too. And even if you try
to gag me, I have written these words
and they are in the mail to all the editors
of the great land where turkeys and bison roam.

# LA VOIX DU PORT

*I invite poets to read every month at Port Au Prince, a Haitian restaurant in Silver Spring, Maryland. The series is called Poetry at the Port. I want voices at all ports of entry to cross over and sing in all the languages that please them. In French. Haitian Creole. Spanish. English. Russian. Turkish. Farsi. Arabic. Tamil. Mandarin. Japanese. All are welcome and nobody requires a visa or even a laisser-passer. One Voice. One World. One Dream.*

*In the French language Haitian weekly, Haiti en Marche, I have a column, also called Poetry at the Port. Each week I present a poem written in Haitian Creole or French and its translation into English. The series of my poems that follows here is from that column.*

****

## Revolutionary Thought: Overheard

"My idea is not complicated, dear foreigner:
Haiti as the center of the universe and Creole

the official language for all authorities,
United Nations, International Criminal Court,

for all kinds of crimes, and NASA as well
because, as you surmise, to fight future wars

we will need codes that not everybody knows . . .
which is why I am leaving Creole with you: your call:

as code language, to explore space. for new commands
in war. Dearest Haiti. Great country, center of my head."

****

## Haitian Conundrums

Rum, nuts and cod at the Diederich house,
and a conversation about the young,

how one in three Haitians are under fifteen,

and how can they know of the sorcerer

who lived in the palace, of the pleasures
and sorrows of exile, of the murdered

in Fort Dimanche, disappeared from earth
like bones moved from Petionville's cemetery,

but 300,000, rubbed out by the earthquake,
are still part of near-term memory,

which we sift, sipping drinks. and sharing
disparate worlds (New Zealand, Ireland,

Sri Lanka, Haiti, the United States, in war
and love) meeting on Hispaniola to weigh

domestic and global variations of Man eating
from his own yard or from his national granary:

in Port au Prince, *partout*, similar questions
of politics and excess, but, dare I say it,

this Haiti has its particular *loas* and ways,
inscrutable to the untrained analyst,

unschooled in history, who cannot appreciate
the irony, of a fort, a killing field, called Sunday.

****

## *Injustice*

To know this country,
when you palaver with people
in the street, you will discover
all kinds of lies, histories
and certainly those
who have experienced
dictatorship, and afterwards
leadership by a priest,
a musician, paradise

or carnival, while
the international community
tries to understand with a belt-
tightening plan what escapes
like a plastic bag into the sea.

****

## *We Are Spirit. We Are King.*

You cannot deny my identity.
I am there even if I am not there.
I am in your head, in the memory
of the country. Even if you have
never met me I am there because
my Sri Lankan brothers
served on the island
as UN Peacekeepers. You know
the whole world came to Haiti
to save us from the gangs?
The island is very important,
a responsibility of foreign countries.
Once, we produced profits
greater than the 13 British
colonies in America.
We have a history
that makes us proud,
a culture, dance, music,
spirits in our own style.
We are not like other islands
We are not broken down,
broken up. We are Haiti.
We are proud. We say hello
with our head held up. Identity
is the most important therapy,
an aid, a tool to reply to the sea
when it decides to rage
against us, to drown
everything. It cannot destroy
this pride in our head.

****

## Crossroads Miami/Port Au Prince

I don't have electricity. I cannot
listen to your radio program.
What did you want to say
to the public? We are neighbors,
brothers, we build a bridge
together as we have
a lot of traffic to manage
between our countries:
musical traffic, dance
and poetry traffic. Yes, yes,
all of this comes with
the cliché that all traffic
includes trafficing off jams.
But I want to know now
if you wish to suggest
a practical solution,
a scholarship to pay
for my education,
or if you would invest
in a big business
and name me
a merchant of dreams
in the crossroads
between Miami
and Port Au Prince,
between this poem
and the current lost
in the broken generator
from the Electricity
Board of Haiti?

****

## The Avocado Season Is Over

The season of avocados
is over. The most beautiful
girl in town is about to marry
a man across the water.

My brother is busy
with his manuscript.
Time to share ideas
in a book has gone
to the country without
a hat. Accept reality.
Don't live anymore
in fantasy.
You are getting along
in years but have only
spoken Creole for two.
You have
a great long life
ahead. Think. Reflect. Tell
all the new families
Congratulations
Good luck. Then
write again about
your life in Haiti
when the avocado
was in bloom.

****

## Free Mind

I am calling all vagabonds, the loose-moraled,
easy women, the entire world to meet this evening
at my house. We must write a letter, even a draft law
for the assembly of deputies, senators with spouses
and children, their heads straight.
Everybody is a person.

If we love to dance, smoke, make love often,
and variously, it is for us to decide, and for us to name
our business. From this day forward our vocabulary
will eliminate all reference to the way people live.
Life is expensive. The head of our bed is large.

****

## How To Go Home

My skin burned on the motorcycle's muffler
when I got on board to go to your house. It was only
the second time I saw the city from the people's
point of view, that I felt skin under my clothes,
that I looked straight at the teeth of the fruit seller,
that anybody passing could have grabbed me
as I sat outside the bulletproof window of the big
suburban that climbs and descends every day
on the mountain road. Every person is a person
with a need to go home, to eat, motorcycle available.

FOR WALT

## Setting Off

Walt explodes on impact in the mind. Nothing becomes everything,
    everything nothing,
the equation turned inside out: poems, democratic practice, phrenology,
    the discovery
of India. There is no pebble from under which Walt does not peep out. I
    fell in love
with him again at the Walt Whitman rest stop on the New Jersey
    Turnpike. I wanted
to call a book Giant Blow Up Walt Whitman Doll. He retired in Camden,
    nursed the wounded
in Washington, walked up and down Paumonok, Manhattan and Staten
    Islands, across
Brooklyn, Queens and the Bronx. He became our first American
    walking poet,
and the most photographed of his time. He gave me license to loaf, to
    lime, to go everywhere
my heart wanted and now that I have come back to stay, he invites me
    to go again.

****

## This Is Not

This is not about Walt Whitman. Not about his beard, his eye, his breath.
    This is not about
his peering behind the tomatoes. This poem does not give a damn that
    he set off from Paumanok
and ended up dressing the wounds of the union dying. And the
    confederate dying, because
he was spotted in my dream—or was it another salt and pepper beard—
    across enemy lines. He was
indeed a contradiction: man, woman, man-woman, peasant, banker,
    slave, free man. He was too
young to call himself gay, too old to call himself gay, too circumspect,
    too metaphoric. But he wrote
*how you settled your head athwart my hips and gently turn'd over*
    *upon me,/And parted the shirt*
*from my bosom-bone, and plunged your tongue to my bare-stript*
    *heart, And reach'd till you felt*

*my beard, and reach'd till you held my feet.* He was American and he wrote
    of places
as far as his imagination could travel. So India became his subject
    and the Moon and the stars.

****

## Advice from Paumanok

Stretch your bones and exercise your muscles. Let a masseuse twirl
and unfurl them. Be sinewed. Limber. Then set off from Paumanok
and go down eventually to the Aguila Islet, via the Panama Canal,
along the coast from Colombia to Peru to Chile. Ricardo Reyes
is waiting to serve you tea in Parral. He will grow up to be
Pablo Neruda. When you are in Central America, make sure
you spend time with Ruben Dario in Managua. Ruben is a blue poet

waiting for you to infuse his pioneering line in Spanish American verse.
You wrote of course about a passage to India. Go there this time.
On Emirates or Air India. Get to know the descendants
of Ramanujan and Kolatkar.  And if you have time, stop
by another long island, Ceylon, known now as Sri Lanka.
I will wait for you there, as if you are a lost uncle, Tambimuttu
returned home from naming Fitzrovia, founding *Poetry London*.
I will unleaf a lamprey for you, the meats sweetened
by the banana skin.  I will adopt your name Walt just
in case I need a calling card to make good in America.

****

## The Walt Whitman Laundromat

The laundry is calling. The post has to be sorted, market mailers trashed,
My life rolls forward. The creeper creeps in the way of the front door,
its sister climbs the Southern wall. The Sun will be detained and deflected
by blinds, the neighbor landscapes his front yard, and I am writing
these lines to assure one more for Walt, one more for the fevered dream
waking up early morning to study the leaves in memory, the ones
that inspire the waking consciousness, to rise abroad, to keep on walking
into this afternoon, now, to sit and give a reading. The laundry, by the way,

remains neglected in the hamper,  and the creeper is unaware of the need
to extract from everything that moves an ode to Walt Whitman.

****

## *Going Home*

I walked with Walt in an earlier age of cool, when we sat on the tin-can banana dock
with Allen and Jack, when we wandered about the tomatoes in the supermarket,
when we set off from Paumanok looking for a passage to India. Those were quieter
times even though Moloch was riding roughshod over us and the best minds
fried on acid and wandered about tenement halls searching for the hipster.
I was young in the city and Allen told me to take care of my economy, to work
in the day and write at night. He was my Jewish uncle and Walt, our patriarch
and matriarch, with his deliciously specific yet indeterminate observations
about love and sex. He nursed everybody, his testament today, his 200th
birthday, when everybody says his name, I go back to my birthplace, out
of the cradle endlessly rocking, turning the pages of my first leaves of grass.

# THE MIGRANT STATES

## America Revisited

The pursuit of happiness, America the Beautiful, home, home
on the range where deer and antelope, in God we trust, down

in Jamaica, Queens, Little Colombia, up in Dutch Harlem, from sea
to shining city on the hill, the light which moves rag-tag ruffians

to band together and fight their dictator, America
which allowed Allen to put his queer shoulder

into the harmonium pressing out songs of innocence
and experience, and gave me a passport, a new set

of associations, America, land of the free, of disaffected
purveyors of persecuted religions living as democrats

and republicans in the new Athens where the foreign-born
can compete for everything except the presidency,

America, dream and door still not wide open, tea party
nay-saying, railing against government by elected

representatives and paying for roads and bridges,
not to mention standing armies. Ay America,

its obligations as part of NATO and the United Nations.
America, that will act when necessary against

evil when it demonstrates against American interests
and those of fellow nations, America the officious

and kind, meddlesome neighbor, the one who stood
by on the sidelines when bombers and rapists broke

into the dwellings of the uppity population
of more than one country, the quarrelsome minority

who had fought for liberty at all costs, this America
contradictory, America, my battle hymn, fifty states

and various dependencies, America bruised, beautiful
and a beacon still where a president lusted once

in his heart and told the press about his dilemmas,
America in constant tussle between countless

ways to document the multiplication of the blackbird
and dominion of the beetle, the disappearance

of a way of life in the rust belt, houses and
smokestacks silent crumbling into television

cameras, wind blowing bric-a-brac, rolling twigs
again over the dust bowl, America that will send

an astronaut to Mars within my lifetime, where
I will step away when the truck rolls on its side

in the thick fog on the still to be repaired I-95.

## The Migrant's Reply

We have been running for so long. We are tired. We want to rest.
  We don't want
to wake up tomorrow and pack our bags. We have gone 10,000 miles.
  We have
boarded a row boat, tug boat, bus, freight train. We have a cell phone
  and some bread.

Our eyes are dry. Our breath needs washing. What next? You are
  putting up
a wall on your Southern flank? What an irony. The country that
  accepts refugees
does not want us. We qualify. We have scars and our host
  governments hunted

at least some of us. The rest fled in fear. Gangs do not spare
  even the children.
White vans took away our uncles, our cousins. Do you think they
  have been made
into plowshares? Ay, what are you saying? Too easy. Too easy to
  wear our hearts

in these words, in slings, on our faces, furrowed, perplexed.
  What happened
to kindness to strangers? Why do we have to be herded like prisoners, held
in a holding camp? We are human beings and, like you, in safer countries,

we have the same obligation to save ourselves and our children.
  Oh, the children.
Look at them. Give them food and school and a new set of clothes.
  Give them
a chance. Whether you are red or blue the eye of the hurricane does not

discriminate. We are your tumbling weeds, hurling cars,
  flooding banks.  And
we are diggers of the dikes.  We can teach you so many languages
  and visions.
You would learn so much: you would never ever say lock us up.

## The Song Today

I hear you singing. I know your song. You waded
into a dinghy, jumped into a rowboat. You climbed
aboard the freighter. You carry a cell phone and a picture,
a name and a number written in the phone. You will call
on arrival. You will cross desert. You will bypass
the wall. You will pray to God. You will not turn back.

# Underground, 2019

*The runaway slave came to my house and stopt outside.*
*I brought him in, gave him water, filled a tub for his sweated body and*
*bruis'd feet,*
*And gave him a room that enter'd from my own, and gave him some*
*coarse clean clothes,*
*And remember perfectly well his revolving eyes and his awkwardness,*
*And remember putting plasters on the galls of his neck and ankles;*
*He staid with me a week before he was recuperated and pass'd north,*
*I had him sit next me at table, my fire-lock lean'd in the corner.*

—Walt Whitman

I too want to serve on the underground railroad. I have ideas and people
to move along to safe harbor. My Tamils still need shelter, host families.
Peace at home is precarious and spies are everywhere, especially
if you are a student leader, an organizer. I am older now but I have not
forgotten youthful ambitions: a country of my own, where siblings
would run the Electricity Board, the Katcheri, police force, tax department,
and most important the deeds office. Come all ye survivors of war.
I have deeds for you to reclaim, and the corresponding lands. I will ask
my army chiefs to get soldiers out of their hammocks and vegetable plots,
to stop making a healthy living selling produce to the civilians. I will
eliminate watch towers and cut the budget for undercover surveillance.

## At the Altar, Day of the Dead

A delight of these waning days
at year's end has been to tune

into Tamil songs and news from
the island, to dream again about

M.G.R and swashbuckling Madrasi
films we used to devour as children;

to each his own the book prescribes,
let us have feast days and bury our dead

with proper libations. Why should
we forget? Memory keeps us tied

to roots, helps sort out unpleasant
fate from the pullulating dance of life,

that we are here still despite
the goonda's dream, to sweep

us into the sea.  I am told this is old hat,
to get a life, move on, such beaten

phrases, whose life, my friend?
Where shall I move?  I am eating

now, preparing body and mind
for the long night without my beloved.

# Cycling

Periyapappa used to listen
to the Tamil Service
on a transistor radio

all afternoon, resting
in his single bed,
or at a desk,

during his long
retirement. He lived
into his 90s for the purpose

of this poem, I don't
recall now whether death
took him a few years shy

of that magic number,
it does not matter.
My friend says you talk

of leaving Sri Lanka at eight
but it seems to me you are
living there still, peeling

rambutans, diving
into the sea while
motorbikes surround

your editor-in-chief
at the intersection
before murdering him,

leaving you and a motley
family, liberal, gentle,
educated to let the fly buzz

in its orbit, snake slide
through the grass to fulfill
its role in the play, eat rats

and battle the mongoose,
trap Man only when
he walks unaware through

the night and steps
on a mine that rears
and bites his leg or hand.

Let us find antidotes fast,
stanch venom, suck
it out or cut off the limb

as necessary, at least Man
will live to hop about
his garden and eat mangos,

rambutans, supervise
his property, listen
to the transistor radio

until death moves him
along to the next battlefield
or garden of delights.

# Baila . . . Your Troubles Away

Folks at home
love "Sea Cruise"

and saving
the last dance

for you.
Their eyes

become stars
humming

"Greensleeves"
before breaking

out on the floor
to "Rock Around

the Clock" and
"Living on Tulsa

Time." They ask:
*have you ever*

*been lonely,*
*have you ever*

*been blue?*
They dance

to tunes
from abroad

but really
go batty

when baila
spins

from inside
the drum

and coconuts
drop

on our head.
Aiyo, machan,

wear a hat,
clap hands,

shake hips
baila, baila.

## At Your Service

Islanders always like to baila,
party, party, nibble the ear

whispering, pump themselves
with arrack and go courting

on the Green, but in these
holidays at year's end

dedicated to forgetting
the war and all those gadflies

buried in graves, some families
mourn their heroes away

from the headlights' glare
of vans— without license plates—

that remain in service waiting
to be summoned when necessary.

## Family Fish

You call my father Uncle
so I have now acquired
a cousin, which cheers

me up as like most
Ceylonese I enjoy
enlarging the family

feast. This one
I suppose is
bittersweet given

our penchant
for early retirement
via bomb drop

from clouds or
roadside device,
but as you say

we have been
released
from interminable

war although
other cousins
linger in rehab

and fishermen from
the neighborhood
are noosed

and dragged
from their boats;
oh these unpleasant

news reports, denied
of course, still cause
the baila singer

to pause. After all,
he too likes prawns
and king fish and frets,

what if fishermen
walk off their decks
and leave

their business
to the Chinese,
will our supply

be assured
after the Forbidden
City has been fed?

## Letter to Galle
*—for the festival*

I sent a poem
but have not yet
had a reply.
I believe the editors

are travelling
or perhaps
they have landed
in the free state

of Galle
for the festival;
I don't know
if to go or stay,

afternoon teas
with poetry seem
the right way to set
mood and wet palate

before celebratory
readings
by prose stars
in the evenings

and then a few
drinks and to bed,
waking up to morning
panel discussions

where the unpleasant
but necessary
subject of domestic
rights will be aired

with no restrictions,
even for the cameras;
how could I miss
the sea breeze

and hot prawns,
imbibe that rare air
blown by special
bellows during

the few days
when Galle
becomes Berlin
after the Wall

came down,
at least, for
ticketed customers
and scholarship

students.  In the end,
even freedom of
expression must be
paid for by somebody.

Yet, I digress.
There are journalists
in hiding and/or
dead.


Note: *Galle, Sri Lanka, hosts an English language literature festival every year.*

# Doubles, Via Taxi

"You want some curry, let us
see whether there is roti still
by Saint Helena; it is evening
and the cooks are tired, eaten
out, you may need to make do

with doubles, that veggi roti,
channa and aubergine, folded
over and sweet, though you can
add some pepper; it was all cane
here once, now grass grown over—

oil booms down south—government
broke the cane industry, but we all right;
you see that hardware shop?
It is rented out; I live upstairs, and
everywhere you look a cousin,

but my son is finishing university
in New York, my sisters are here.
If you had come Saturday I would
have brought you by a grand Hindu
wedding, my niece's. Come again.

I will take you by the Big Man Leroy's
place, what he call Legacy House,
in Wellsprings, and then over
to Queens Park Oval, the old city,
*Miguel Street*, wherever you dream, Mon."

# The Golden Poem

Walking in the plaza of Puerto Maldonado reciting a poem about lovers
in the New York subway, evening breeze suggesting a windbreaker,
laughter in the speech of the town after work, couples nuzzling under
ceiba trees, and the seller of rolled whirls of sugar and dough engaging

a boy in wide-eyed chat, you and I walking a poem out as one walks a dog,
to give it time to smell and explore, to exercise its limbs and rights
in the communal square, where it can take root and become
  a gathering place
for humans and bats and birds, a statue in stone to the Poem, whose
  obsidian eyes

will not be stolen for a souvenir by a visiting writer and rival whose
  jealousy extends
even to the fringes of the Amazon,  if not pilfered earlier by a thief
  with economic
goals, a migrant perhaps from the Andes or coast, who will turn
  the eyes into cash
before setting up the miner's sluice gate and mercury supply by
  the riverbank.

## Rescue, Lima

I got a head start, Mervyn,
wrote through the night,
the neighbor's party
blaring through the window,

but poetry had invited me
to dance, and despite
the noise, tapped
its peculiar drum, allowing

me to go liming across
all the boundaries;
I don't believe certainly
in terrestrial limits,

soul must fly; cannot
decompose with
the perishable heart.
Love revives even

in wilderness, shoots
green across once
barren land; in
my vision I visited

Iceland to witness
rescue of its collapsed
hills, Lima's dust
blows through morning,

loudspeakers have
shut down, neighboring
rats gone to bed,
and I to dream.

# Lima, January

It is summer here,
hot for the moment,

plantain tree bearing fruit
in the garden, passion and

mango in the shops, a lot
of fish, the country blessed

by the Humboldt Current
which brings cold water

from the Antarctic and
plentiful anchovies with it

to feed up the food chain
(including Man).  Grey Lima

sky where you don't see
the sun, but not as true

where we live in La Molina
high above the rest

of the city. Chattering
classes gone to beach

houses, taxi drivers,
bus conductors plying routes

requiring less acrobatics
as many residents are away

on mental holiday attending
meetings, reading horoscopes.

# Discovering Cemex

At Belen by night they drift into dock: pontoons, barges, row boats
with outboard motors, filled with the purple black *acai*, known as
super-berry in the organic food market, crushed and drunk fresh
at the Belen port, trucked to the coast for juice bars where frozen
berries mixed with pineapple or passion, or muscle powder perhaps
for an extra kick, gave me sustenance for a few days in Copacabana.

I have looked for the *acai* in Peru without luck although I noticed
the seeds dried and polished for a necklace at a handicrafts store
in Puerto Maldonado.  Pity the Peruvians have not discovered
the secret of my Rio sojourn, its underground energy, drink
to which I returned from a day spent comparing strategies
to reduce one's carbon footprint, and felt refreshed with hope

that my Brazilians, lovers of Amazon fruits, would not squander
their wealth in piercing the sandy floor for oil, or churning
it up with water, for gold. *Sustainable* is the word,
like plastics at the time of *The Graduate*, and second growth
can support complex biodiversity if allowed to prosper
in peace. There are signs of recovery even in former pits

mined to make cement. Let us grow forest cover around
abandoned rubber plants in the jungle, at *Fordlandia*, in the peat
highlands three hours from Bogota,  so one day an intrepid
explorer among our descendants will hack away at centuries
of thick foliage to discover another *Angkor Watt*, or *Polonnaruwa*,
the once state-of-the art factory of the *Cemex* Corporation.

# DEPARTURES

# Getting Over Suicide

You say nobody writes ten poems in a day, but my personal best
is seven I protest, and I am under observation, and there are no sharp

objects, or even long sheets to twist, to escape through the window,
or to be strung to the ceiling, a bit of old hat
   I admit, the
      rhetorical suicide,

various advance announcements, but nobody lends much weight
to warnings, the poet Ruiz Udiel, who just expired in Managua, hanged,

after drinking wine with friends, published a poem about how the suicides
Sexton, Plath and Pizarnik were born four years apart, one after the other;

now to the question if extensive and early perusal of the text would
have prevented him from dying to welcome the New Year of 2011,

we shall of course, as always, remain in the dark, nursing the vast,
empty sacks in our hearts where sadness flowers for hours, and days,

at birth and death anniversaries, before expiring as well, allowing
us to recover and celebrate life and birth once again.

## Alastair, Gone

You have left the field to wild grass,
creepers, bracken, nests popping
out from branches. I don't know

if you ride caboose in Temuco now,
or step out with moorhens
and grouse, or into that Dominican

plot which you tilled, says McGrath,
with your farmer's hands. I don't know
of course is just a fiction,

an invention, a hedge, a way to grieve.
You are dead, I read, who named
my secret country,

then disappeared, as was your practice
throughout life, the New Yorker office
your only secure address, to which

I wrote often, and from which you emerged
to invite me to a fejoada, to say, pare
the poem, to begin on the lines

*you must love*, and end on the verse
from where I greet you today,
*the other side of the sea.*

# Departures

Jose Carlos Mendes expired in Monterrey, Francisco Udiel
in Managua, now Adam Zameenzad, you are leaving Lima.

You say the heat this summer bothered you too much,
you could not breathe, you feared a stroke. The vegetable

powder from the Andes picked up at market you ate too much
of it, the smelly fish entered your subconscious, I salute

your valor to have given up the comforts of Shant Cottage
to experiment in Lima with another version of the heat

you left behind in Pakistan under a different name which
I have let go from my mind. You are baptized after all

as Adam and my curiosity about your age and passport
has not been satisfied in a prosaic way though you write

cogent, passionate sentences, and I can go to bed
blissfully and finally disinterested, carrying a Zameenzad

novel or poem to keep me company. Writers are lucky,
their words embedded in friends via email and book.

## Manslaughter

Key of course is the aggressor's intention, whether on boarding the ship
he meant to shoot four bullets into the brain of his victim, but in the crossfire
other bullets may have been responsible, and then "whose victim" becomes
the question. There is a reduction in the evidentiary standard in a situation
of chaos, individual agency is swept up in the beating storm, and nothing can
or should be proved but all will be left in varying states of anger and resolve—
like the parents of Rachel Corrie who wait still for accounting from the driver
of the bulldozer but that was some time ago and Rachel lives on in her foundation,
a play, and now a ship diverted from its desired port of call; and yes I know
these lines appear to take sides as if such considerations need to be raised
to determine guilt and mete punishment when manslaughter is still manslaughter
whether in Gaza or Tel Aviv or Teheran; I mean the subjects are corpses and the
question is how to bury the bodies under what laws and with what compensation.

# The Old Yankee Jesus

I am glad to see you have kept your faith,
that Jesus is holding for you on the third rail,
that a life of subways and the M-104 Bus
have kept you honest and dreaming reasonable
goals, such as cadging a seat at Old Yankee
Stadium a bit late but a warm-your-behind
nonetheless, a bet on the future when Jesus
threw a perfect game and hot dogs cost a nickel.

## Currency
*—for A.Z.*

I meant to write again
about Taprobane
but your imminent
departure from Lima

insists on a few lines.
We have spoken
over twenty years
of the sometimes

bitter divisions
between various
classes and
phenotypes

of men but as
you say we are
all browned
by the same Sun,

rained upon
from clouds, seeded
or left to capture
naturally what

oceans evaporate,
we are guided
by politicians and
priests and teachers,

or none of the above,
at least we consult
with doctors,
whether herbalist

or radiologist,
we have numerous
ways of getting
somewhere closer

to the right call
for health, wealth
happiness, and coping
as well with this inevitable

sadness woken up
after such a long time
and plentiful conversation
realizing the journey

is all and friends give
shelter even in the attic
and that money is
currency principally

to fill the table, furnish sheets,
so we can eat and sleep
and talk easily while we still
have time before the taxi arrives.

## Koan for Jim

What to write about a man who stayed
behind the lines to make sure the lines
were secure, the house strong, that it merited
attention of President and Secretary,
a man who acted faster and more completely
than our sometimes contrary host.

Jim, you deserve a koan, a zen teaching.
Be silent in public; don't let visiting birds
steal the jewels owing  to some careless
gesture. Carry them in your bones,
your industry. Carry them forward
while securing your behind.

# Babylonian Song
—for J.K.

When José talked of his writing practice,
inventing a poem each day, the 6,000 and
counting he has gathered in folders, backed
up on stand-alone hard drives, I was impressed

by the majesty of ambition and his commitment
to resolution of dilemmas through summoning
his Muse, Guadalupe, but I used to mutter
the mischievous question, what kind of Babel

is this man trying to build, why the confident
announcing of numbers, accumulation of bricks,
what will the fat line he baptized for the new
Baroque poets produce for the rest of the guild,

the ones who still conceive lyrics, who believe
that fishmongers and accountants alike
speak and read poetry, that there is a bridge
upon which we can all stride over the Seine

or Thames, the Niger, or Nile, the Amazon,
to meet our lovers or publishers, the eternal
reader who will be patient even with human
ambition, the tower that leans but does not

fall, the Cantos that could not sustain
the force of Ezra Pound's energy, his creative
wave breaking at times unnoticed except
when he pulled himself up out of his song

and said, pull down thy vanity, Paquin, pull down?

# First Holy Communion
### —for Anandan, May 10, 2003

The host at St. James on Spanish Place, London
was grainy wheat, pocked with yeast, broken
off the loaf  while the wafer raised over the bright
white stone of St. Rita's in Wellington, Florida
before a smorgasbord of immigrants is whiffle-thin.

But none of this matters, God's manifest even
in air, I know this as I know the hunger woken up
by that thick, brown Jamesian wedge, the child's meat
that built my spirit . . . Son, let me give you the hunger,
pass you this bread—it is blest—and like Joseph

the diplomat retires now to the eaves, yet walks up
the aisle with your mother who led you through
these years of instruction, with whom we adventured
breaking bread throughout the globe, the shape
of this host, the circle of this light.

# Summer, Chess (for Anandan)

You go now and I am sad,
and the sadness will spill
into late summer
and autumn until we meet
again when the leaves
fall and chestnuts
smack our memories
alive, and you ask

Dad, did
you always walk
in Regent's Park
when leaves turned
red and yellow, and
the morning bristled
and the sun seared
yet left your skin cold?

A cold sun, Dad,
I feel it too. This
summer that I thought
would go slow
has turned now
into a sprinter's dash,
and what's to do. Yes,
write and fill

days with friends,
and games, and sums,
until next summer,
until the next time
we go to bed and know
there's no morning flight,
and your queen and rook
are ready to trap my king.

## Morning Mass, Halloween (for Lola)

Hushed tones. Place of worship. Early morning. A woman kneeling
in the pew could not get up. The priest brought her communion; then
another parishioner called for an ambulance. The fireman, a friend
of the ambulance driver, arrived in his fire truck. They work together
naturally. What to do now? Walk to the font, dip fingers in holy water,
then go out to my car. Paramedics will lay her on a stretcher, pump
her heart, wheel her away to the hospital. Life is coming to its end:
a repeat. In my dad's case his heart stopped while he kneeled at a pew.
Nobody could revive it. He would have loved to see my daughter,
smiling as she guards the witch's cauldron this Halloween, sweets in hand.

FOR WALT

## Lilacs at Walt's Home

The Whitman house stands, yes, and there are period
furnishings inside the rooms, birthing bed, spinning wheel,
chamber pots. But only one chair survives from the Whitman
family, all the rest travelled to Brooklyn when Walt turned three,
and then were handed down, disposed, sold. Can we reconstruct
the history of the furniture, as well as the poems, the various
drafts of *Leaves of Grass*? Not every nut and screw, armchair,
bellows can be rescued from the inexorable oblivion called time.
But a few pieces, yes, the chair Walt sat on, and the wavy glass panes,
through which one sees the lilacs as if they were weeds in a deep sea
garden, swaying, waving from 1819 to 2019, two hundred years on,
bicentennial for Walt and the lilacs last in the dooryard bloom'd.

****

## The Emotion Again

I ask the panel, the audience: what next? We have finished
celebrating Walt Whitman's 200th birthday. Who will lead us
into the next century? Do we find the driver in our own batteries,
energy coursing through cells from foods we eat for body and mind,
like this delicious feast finished now, ten days at summer's beginning
to honor the founder of our republic of letters, not the first but the most

expansive American, who stretched his imagination to encompass
the continent and travelled beyond, to India, to the Moon, Sun and stars,
into the interior constellations in a leaf of grass. Walt Whitman,
we do not want the party to end. We wish to keep stroking
your grey beard, reading the day's news out loud as you lay dying
in Camden, bedridden, reported on almost daily by the *Times*,

if you had drunk milk punch, broth, and twice when you seemed
to have kicked the bronchial pneumonia, eaten a mutton chop.
You dropped out of the news too when the paper thought
you had improved enough to live without their noting
every food and visitor, brother George, sister in law,
biographer, favorite niece Jessie, and your final physician

Doctor McAllister, your last words a request to attendant
Fritzinger: *Warry, Shift*. Roll over Walt Whitman. You told
the doctor—who asked if you were in pain— no, almost
inaudibly, a wisp of smoke floating out of the row house
into the street, mixing with the air, falling later on as rain,
in poems and songs recollected in tranquility again and again.

****

## *Gone from Paumanok*

I feel I must end with a bang, at least a shake and a whistle,
a riff, a taste, a dance on a dime. I want to end because
suites must finish, poems arrive at the punch line, the final
full stop. I am not sure if I can go on like the sea, ridden
with plastics, with patches dead even to oxygen. I am not
sure I can whirl in space like a meteor, an asteroid
or some rubbish from a failed satellite. I am not after all
a celestial body, or a golden sunflower, just a fifty-eight-
year-old man a few hundred miles from Paumanok
and stopped—owing to family ties, to work and the need
to build a house, high enough to avoid the rain when it floods.

"Migrant States is a book where passion and memory meet, a book that calls for open borders of the mind, it is a book that knows that everyone and no one is a foreigner on this planet and that the country of the poets has no customs. With Whitman as his interlocutor, Indran Amirthanayagam takes us on the journey with no return, where our ticket is a moving and beautiful song."

—Ilya Kaminsky, author of Deaf Republic and Dancing in Odessa

ॐ

Indran Amirthanayagam was born in Sri Lanka but he's certainly American-made. When ideals are shattered, poetry saves; and this book conveys truth from a master storyteller representing the high tradition of poetry with dignity and conviction throughout this powerful collection; and there are no better poems of Walt Whitman than are found here. Amirthanayagam's voice is a sword of light. *"Speak to me. We have/ little time. Though the sun/ will explode long after/ we've disappeared."*

—Grace Cavalieri Maryland Poet Laureate

ॐ

An activist poet is rooted in revolutionary change as opposed to a "literary"-poet who, like Auden, believes that a poem "does nothing." It just survives. Sri Lankan-born Indran Amirthanayagam, who writes poetry in 5 languages (Haitian, Spanish, French, Portuguese and most of all in American-English), is one of the truly great activist poets in these United States. Read this book and I've no doubt you'll agree with me.

—Jack Hirschman, emeritus Poet Laureate of San Francisco

ॐ

In *Recalling Sundays*, Indran begins, "I have fought the blues on so many Sundays...". It locates him immediately: his ear for the language, the jazz of these 'migrant states', and his emotional condition, as one of so many in exile. In powerful poems that testify to the will to live, he intersperses verses he wrote to celebrate Walt Whitman, the keeper of the American Ideal. Indran is of like mind, believing that in the monastery of poetry, in the fields of the imagination, "the dragon of reality might follow, to be slain". In *Beating*, he writes, "...when this poem goes off the road/spins wheels in the mud...". It is with such gifted lines, such joy in the performance of duty, that this poet allows the metaphor its chance to create a Heaven, that remind the migrant states of the promise they once held, that poetry still holds in its ability to combat the blues.

—Mervyn Taylor, author of *Voices Carry*